Arduino: 2 Books In 1

— — — — — ❧☙❧☙ — — — — —

Inside you will find:

<u>Arduino:</u>
The Comprehensive Beginner's Guide to Take Control of Arduino Programming

<u>Arduino:</u>
Best Practices to Excel While Learning Arduino Programming

Arduino

───── ✥✥✥✥ ─────

The Comprehensive Beginner's Guide to
Take Control of Arduino Programming

Miles Price

liable for any hardship or damages that may befall them after undertaking information described herein.

Additionally, the information in the following pages is intended only for informational purposes and should thus be thought of as universal. As befitting its nature, it is presented without assurance regarding its prolonged validity or interim quality. Trademarks without written consent and can in no way be considered an endorsement from the trademark holder.

Table of Contents

Introduction

Congratulations on downloading *Arduino* and thank you for doing so.

The following chapters will discuss how to start programming for the Arduino, and how to quickly and efficiently become a competent programmer.

There are plenty of books on this subject on the market, thanks again for choosing this one! Every effort was made to ensure it is full of as much useful information as possible, please enjoy!

Chapter 1:
What Is Arduino?

Heads up — it's the twenty-first century. It's easier than ever to make your own gadgets. The Arduino is a hardware and software package that allows you to create your own gadgets from scratch. It's essentially a microcomputer that you can hook all sorts of neat things up to and that you can make full-fledged projects out of.

Programming your Arduino projects isn't terribly difficult, but there are a lot of underlying concepts that you need to grasp if you really want to propel yourself forward as a programmer. You're going to be working with pretty low-level concepts, so it's important that you familiarize yourself with all of these before you jump into Arduino programming.

Do note that this book follows the path of C to C++ to the Arduino framework, which is generally considered the best path for somebody who wants to become an Arduino programmer.

Buckle in, we're going to be on this road for a while!

Chapter 2:
C Programming — An Introduction

Before we get into anything else in this book, we're going to spend some time learning the logic of programming. As somebody wanting to work with Arduino, it's going to be of the utmost importance that you spend time actually learning the logic behind programming. While Arduino programming can yield you some really cool results, the *programming* part is incredibly important, and you can't really expect to do much with your Arduino rig if you're clueless as to just what you're capable of doing as a programmer!

Moreover, without a firm foundation in programming, you're going to be pretty much lost moving forward. Many aspects of Arduino programming will leave you fundamentally lost if you don't understand the underlying programming logic.

While many Arduino units are *capable* of working with any language that can be compiled to machine code compatible with Arduino, you will get the most mileage out of learning C and C++. This is because the Arduino framework is actually just based on C and C++. It's actually a library. Moreover, if you have a firm understanding of these two languages, then your path going forward is much clearer because you'll be ready to take on bigger programming challenges and full-fledged projects. Because Arduino and C/C++ are so heavily integrated with one another, you have access to a lot of system features that you may not have access to otherwise, and you can really get down and dirty with the system to make the most of the tools which are available to you.

So let's start with the C programming language. First, what is the C programming language, and what is the reason for why Arduino is so closely intertwined with it? Well, to start with the very basics, the C programming language is pretty much the go-to for anything that gets down and dirty with systems architecture in this day and age. Since the Arduino is more or less a microprocessor, this is pretty much exactly what you want.

But what makes the C language so good for this specific purpose? To understand this, we need to take a little trip into the past. The C programming language is very old. In fact, it's almost forty years old! The first version of the C programming language was written sometime at AT&T's Bell Labs sometime in the late 1970s, chiefly by a guy named Dennis Ritchie, though with the rest of the Bell Labs team pitching in as well. It served as a continuation of the already existing programming language B, which in itself was a continuation of the programming language BCPL.

However, it also changed the paradigm for programming languages quite a bit by offering a large amount of functionality and features that hadn't been majorly present in other languages before, or at least not to the extent that they were featured in C. For example, there were a variety of new data types that hit the scene with C that weren't present in the language B, which only had a singular data type. This meant that many more types of data could be stored and manipulated with a greater amount of ease.

Additionally, C received a large amount of support from the developers, with the development of a huge number of different libraries and assets intended to make C an extremely easy and functional language to use, regardless of who was trying to use it.

Beyond simple reasons of functionality, though, C gained traction because of one other major factor: the popularity of Unix systems. Unix was an operating system also developed at Bell Labs. It gained a lot of popularity for a few key reasons. The first of which was the fact that it was quite accessible. People never really had to try too hard to use and understand a Unix system, especially in comparison to the other primary computing interfaces of the day. Moreover, because of the low licensing cost, and the fact that it would run on many different hardware configurations, Unix became the operating system of both business and academia. It was cost efficient, easy to use, and easy to license.

C gained more popularity thanks to, firstly, the fact that Unix would come packaged with a C compiler, but also thanks to the fact that Unix was eventually rewritten from the ground up in the C programming language, showing the true effectiveness at C and the real usefulness of it as a language.

Unix became far more popular as time pressed on and so would C, as the language began to catch on. The thing about C was that not only was it fantastic in terms of system programming, but it held a lot of general usability in the fact that the language put many of the things that you needed to understand right in front of you. For example, data types were relatively easy to understand compared to other languages of the time. The manner in which functions were set up and used was relatively straightforward as well.

So, in the end, C would see a massive expansion in terms of overall usage. As time progressed, the language would use its massive influence to have an impact on many other languages. These languages include but aren't limited to its immediate descendant C++ as well as Java, C#, Python, Perl, Lua, and any number of other languages that are commonly used today.

Despite the fact that so many languages were massively influenced by C, none would ever be so as effective at combining readability with raw power. In fact, C is widely considered as the language that is only one step above the raw language used to talk to microprocessors, *Assembly*, in terms of abstraction. Abstraction is a concept that we'll go into greater detail on when we hit the chapter concerning C++ and discuss object-oriented programming concepts, but for now, just understand abstraction as the idea of things being made simpler and less difficult to use, to understand, and to unintentionally mess up.

Anyhow, because C so efficiently combines raw power and readability, it is the best starting point for you as a hopeful Arduino programmer. In essence, the best path forward for you is to start at C and really learn what's going on below the hood in computer programming. From there, you can move on to C++ and learn some of the more abstract concepts. Afterward, you should be able to quickly and easily pick up all of the information that you need to in terms of Arduino programming by looking at the Arduino terminology, learning about the current state of Arduino projects, and looking at the available code for the Arduino interface.

So, moving on, let's start working with C. To work with C, you're going to probably want what's called an IDE. IDE stands for an integrated development environment, and there are a lot of different options that you can choose from. All of them have their own sets of advantages and disadvantages, and there is no clear-cut choice. However, you're almost certainly going to want one that comes with a C compiler.

What is a compiler?

This is the first major lesson that we have to hit in this book. Essentially, computers do not understand English. That much should really go without saying. They have no real way to grasp the language or to truly what's going on when we try to communicate with them. Another consequence of this is despite how we may try, computers, in the end, will only understand machine code. On a level below that, too, computers understand solely systems of ones and zeroes, known as binary. So what you really need is a translator. Compilation serves this purpose.

There are two different ways to run programs: compiled programs and interpreted programs. For the purposes of Arduino programming and learning C/C++, you're only really going to be working with compiled programs so I won't spend much time on what interpreted languages do. Compiled languages, however, essentially convert a program directly into machine code to run on the machine's hardware itself. So essentially, when you compile your code, what you're actually doing is translating it into a language that a computer can read. Easy peasy, right?

Well, not so much. Compilation is straightforward, but programming languages are fickle. You will make a lot of errors, and compilers very much are not forgiving of these sorts of errors. Just be aware of the fact that you will make these errors and have patience going forward.

Anyway, you have to have a compiler in order run C and C++ code, so it's generally just easier to get one with your IDE. Regardless of your platform, though, Eclipse and CLion are both solid choices that offer compiler options as well. A simple Google search will reveal either to you with little to no issue. Be sure that if you do use Eclipse that you won't be confused; while the primary version of Eclipse is renowned for Java development, the IDE itself is multi-purpose and has a lot of utility as a C/C++ IDE as well. You simply have to make sure that you enable the C/C++ features of Eclipse rather than just using the barebones Java version because then you won't be able to do any of the tasks that you need to do, obviously.

If at the end of the day, your IDE of choice doesn't have a C/C++ compiler, then you'll need to poke around to find one that works for your OS. For Unix-like systems such as Linux and macOS, the GCC suite is relatively common. For Windows systems, MinGW is a common choice.

So, with all of that said, let's assume that at this point you have your compiler, and your IDE installed. With all of that done, we can now start to move more into the meat of this lesson, which is actually programming. So, in your IDE of choice,

create a new project or file or whatever you must; the key goal
is that you end up with a blank C file. Go ahead and write the
following within it:

```c
#include <stdio.h>
int main()
{
        printf("hello world\n");
        return 0;
}
```

Then from here, carry out your IDE's procedure for compiling
and running. Normally, it has a preset function that integrates
with your installed compiler to take your file and run it. This is
certainly true for Eclipse and CLion, at least. Anyhow, try to
run the program however you must.

You should see a console screen pop up. Depending upon your
compiler and IDE, it may disappear instantly, or it may stick
around for a moment until you press 'enter' or something of
the like.

On the console, though, it should show 'hello world,' if it did
show, then congratulations, you just wrote your first program.
How cool is that? From here, we're going to work on some
more in-depth concepts and slowly branch out from here to
build a greater understanding of C and C++ concepts.

Values and Variables

The next thing that we're going to need to talk about is 'values and variables.' Values and variables are foundational to pretty much all forms of programming, so having a nuanced understanding of what they are and how they work is pretty much crucial if you want to actually be a programmer.

What is a value?

A value is a little bit hard to define, actually. Remember earlier in the chapter when I mentioned how computers only really understand things in terms of ones and zeroes? Computers parse everything into equations performed upon sets of ones and zeroes referred to as *bytes*. No matter what you feed a computer — whether it's 137938230, 'hello there,' or 3.141569 — they are all understood, at the most basic level, as a series of ones or zeroes.

However, to break all of this down, the computer has to categorize all of these different forms of data into, well, different *forms*. This gives it a standard by which it can compare all of them and make determinations based upon those decisions in particular.

So, we just listed a few different forms that information can take. Essentially, a value just refers to that, information, regardless of the form that it takes. More specifically, it refers to a very specific and pinpointed piece of information. For example, *37* is a value, 'cats' is a value, and so on and so forth.

C categorizes these values into several different types. These types are referred to as *data types*. The following are the most common forms of data types in C:

- **int**

  This data type refers to *integers*, which are essentially just whole numbers.

- **float**

  This data type refers to *floating point numbers*, which are decimals more or less.

- **double**

  This data type refers to double precision numbers, which are also decimals but has a much larger range of numbers. However, this also comes with the tradeoff that doubles take up a far larger amount of data.

- **char**

  This data type refers to *characters*, which are single-byte ASCII representations of symbols. This symbols can be alphanumeric, or they can be special characters such as '!.' Anyone of these symbols, such as 'A,' '3,' or '.' are all stored in a singular byte. We'll get to how this correlates to longer strings of characters at a later point.

Having this framework of data types allows you to perform manipulations upon different values. For example, having an understanding of how integers work allows you to execute arithmetic operations with integers such as addition, subtraction, division, and so forth. But let's say that one wanted more than to just work with a single value. Let's say that one actually wanted to *store* a value. How would one do such a thing?

Well, the way that you can store and manipulate a value is through the creation of something called a 'variable.' It's at this point that we're going to start getting into some more heavy concepts than you're likely used to because a firm understanding of the computer science behind this idea is necessary for being an efficient programmer later on. Understanding the computer science at this point will also make it far easier to understand the abstractions which occur later in this very chapter.

Essentially, when one defines a variable, what they are actually doing is setting aside space within the computer's memory for the value to be kept within. Computers have an active store of memory called their *random access memory* which is intended for on-the-fly storage and retrieval of certain amounts of data. This data is normally that which is intended to be regularly manipulated throughout the program's running. The specifics of this don't matter too much; just understand a few key basics.

Imagine a city's plan. When a new plot of land is designated, space is reserved for a certain address. That address then refers to that plot of land thereafter, regardless of what fills the space. This is similar to the way in which computer memory works. These spaces in the computer's memory are known as

RAM, and the manipulation of this asset can make your programs do a lot more and be a lot more efficient.

Afterward, you can reference the data stored at this location or even manipulate the data directly and change what lives on that proverbial plot of land altogether. Herein lies the utility of variables, the ability to change, assign, and maintain certain values through keeping it in the computer's memory and then changing it after the fact. This means that you can keep important information throughout the running course of the program and change that information as you see fit, too.

In C, when a computer reserves space, what it first looks at is the *type* of the variable. Different data types will take up different amounts of space. We'll talk a little bit more about this here in just a moment, but for now, just understand that this is critical because different data types first and foremost need a certain amount of space reserved and secondly need to interact with other operations within the program in a different way. For example, there is no reason that an integer and a character should be able to be added together.

After this, the variable is then given a name. This name is ultimately up to you. Throwaway variables are, by convention, given names starting with the letter 'i' then working their way up through the alphabet. Other variable names can vary depending upon what function the variable exactly performs and what you're exactly trying to accomplish with the variable. The only thing that a variable name may not contain is special characters, aside from underscores or dashes. This necessarily includes spaces. Your variable names may not include spaces.

After that, you have created the space for the value to be held. Then you need to assign that space a value. You do so through the use of the assignment operator '=.' You then give the value that you want to assign to the variable.

Here is the basic formula:

dataType variableName = value;

Note that it must end with a semicolon. In C and C++, all statements end in a semicolon. A statement is a name for any operation that a computer carries out in an individualistic manner.

If we wanted to create a variable called 'numberOfGuitars' and set it to two, we could do this like so:

int numberOfGuitars = 2;

Note that a value is a value is a value. This means that, as long as the data types match, you can assign a variable the value of another variable. Observe:

int mainVariable = 3;

int placeholder;

// you can create a variable without initializing it, though this isn't recommended.

// Only done here to show the process.

placeholder = mainVariable;

From the line above, *placeholder* would assume the value of *mainVariable*, which is, of course, 3. Now, if we were to

manipulate the variable *mainVariable* and change it to
something else, *placeholder* would retain the original value of
3 until it was likewise manipulated.

Note that you can, as I said, create a variable without
initializing it, or giving it a value. This was done to show that
you *can* do this, which in turn places a greater emphasis on
what the creation of a variable actually does. When we wrote
the line *int placeholder,* we created a space big enough to hold
an *int* variable. This space hadn't been filled yet, but when we
referred to it later, the compiler would have had no issue
interpreting exactly what it was that we were trying to do.

To build a little bit more on the idea of reserved spaces for
variables: let's talk a bit more about data types. There were
some important parts that we skipped over that this book
wouldn't be a complete reference without. Moreover, when
you're working with limited spaces, as you will be on Arduino,
it's important that you have some sort of idea of how space is
allocated.

The biggest thing to note here is that certain types of variables
do have size constraints. For example, the standard integer
can only go from about -32,000 to 32,000. Moving beyond
this amount will actually have it reset to the very bottom of the
bound and then count up from there, not desirable.

However, you can undo these sorts of constraints, or enforce
them, in one of two ways.

The first is by dictating that a data type is *unsigned*. When you
do so, the range is made the same but wholly positive.

Therefore, an unsigned *int* would have the same range of around 65,000, but instead of it consisting of both positive and negative integers, the entire set would be wholly positive ranging up to around 65,000.

The other way is by setting up a *long* variable. *Long* is another data type that takes up two more bytes than a standard integer. However, as a tradeoff from this, you expand your range from around negative two million to positive two million. Moreover, if you were to use an unsigned *long*, you could have a range from zero to roughly four million. The reason that long variables aren't preferred over integers in C is that they take up twice the space in memory, and when you're working with small memory amounts, every byte counts.

Do note that there are also long doubles. While ordinary doubles can go to 15 decimal places, long doubles can go to 19 and can go from roughly $3.4 * 10^{-4932}$ to $1.1 * 10^{4932}$, massive and infinitesimal numbers, as they were.

Arrays

Arrays in C are a very important concept, and for that reason, we're going to try to cover them next. To better understand arrays, think back to our description of how the city is planned. Remember how we brought up that you could reference any given plot of land by a certain address? Bear that in mind as we move forward in the lesson.

Let's say that we wanted to group certain kinds of data together. For example, sometimes, you want to store things of the same value in the same place. It would be unwieldy as a programmer to reference something like:

jakeFirstGrade = 84;

jakeSecondGrade = 97;

jakeThirdGrade = 83;

jakeFourthGrade = 93;

joeFirstGrade = 81;

joeSecondGrade = 73;

joeThirdGrade = 98;

joeFourthGrade = 76;

Not only that, but because of the way that values are stored in the computer's memory, this could actually massively slow down the overall processing speed of your program because instead of things being somewhat grouped together, the computer instead has to reach into different places in random access memory so it can pull up the values that it needs.

Instead, it would be much better if we could group all of a given student's grades into one variable and then access them later. (Actually, it would be better if we could group *all* of the grades together, but we'll talk about that in just a second.)

Well, fortunately, this sort of functionality is very much available, and it exists in the form of arrays.

The way that an array works is that you basically tell the compiler how many plots of land you need to allocate. It will then allocate those plots of land and link them together, that way the entire chain may be easily referenced.

Note that when you define an array, all of the plots of land must be of the same type and size. Let's look at how we would define Jake's grades as an array. An array declaration takes the basic form of:

dataType arrayName[arraySize];

From here, you can also build the array by naming the values within brackets, each value delimited by commas like so:

dataType arrayName[arraySize] = {value1, value2, ... , valueN};

If you don't completely fill in every space, remaining spaces will be left blank. You cannot, however, set more values than the array is set to hold. For example, *valueN* may never be valued *(arraySize+1)*, that is.

If we wanted to set Jake's grades, we could do this like so:

int jakeGrades[4] = { 84, 97, 83, 93 };

And we could set Joe's grades in much the same way. Now, how do we go about accessing this information?

Every value within an array is commonly referred to as an 'element' of the array. The computer accesses the different elements of the array by looking at the address referenced by their specific spot in the array, then retrieving that data.

Computers start counting elements at '0.' This means the first element of an array is element 0. This also means that the last element in an array of *n* size will be element *n-1*. This is yet another relatively straightforward but extremely important lesson to be learned at this point in the book.

You reference a certain element in an array by following this:

arrayName[elementPosition]

For example, to access the first element in *jakeGrades*, we would reference the element at position 0:

jakeGrades[0]

You can then use this to set other values of variables or perform any sort of normal arithmetic operations that you would need:

int placeholder = jakeGrades[0];
        // placeholder's value would be 84

You can also construct two-dimensional arrays. Two-dimensional arrays are best described as something like a spreadsheet, you have your rows, and you have your columns. You can declare a two-dimensional array by doing it this way:

dataType name[rows][columns];

You can also populate these arrays (populate in this case, means 'add values to') when you declare them by nesting brackets. Each set of brackets corresponds to a row, and there are as many nested brackets as there are rows.

With that in mind, how would we create and populate a 'grades' array that contained the data for the two students Jake and Joe? It would look like this example:

grades[2][4] =   {{84, 97, 83, 93], {81, 73, 98, 76}};

With that, you've created an array of students' grades with row 1 being Jake's grades and row 2 being Joe's grades. This can be scaled as large as you would like it to be scaled.

Strings

Having spent a good minute talking about arrays, now is the time that we talk about strings. We will go into strings a little bit more in-depth in the following chapter, but for now, it's good that you have an underlying knowledge of how strings actually work because they will be of paramount importance in almost every programming project you do in the future. Even though languages like C++ and Java massively simplify working with strings, they still work in the same basic manner at their very core, so it's important that we establish exactly how they work.

We talked about the concept of 'characters' as a data type a little bit earlier in the book. It may not have been immediately clear how or why storing a singular character as data may be useful. In fact, in a lot of ways, being able to store a singular character is *not* useful. However, when you combine that utility with the utility of arrays, what you begin to develop is a very powerful duality combining the two that allows you to store long sequences of text.

Everything that you type may be considered a string in its own right. Strings are simply sets of textual information. More accurately, strings refer to *arrays of characters* in the context of fundamental computer science. Working with strings means working, essentially, with sets of characters.

Understand that, moving forward, you can actually develop strings by creating character arrays that are ended with the *null-terminating* character, '\0.'

Again, this is as far as practical knowledge of arrays in C really goes for the purposes of working with Arduino. Strings will be covered in a wider context when we get to the C++ chapter and start discussing the standard template library.

Pointers

One of the biggest parts of C's raw utility is the fact that it allows you to directly manipulate many things that other languages don't really bother letting you touch. One of these things is the stuff going on under the hood in the random access memory or *RAM*. This is important is because if you want to have the most efficient program possible, you're going to need to alter memory addresses. Moreover, because of the way that C and C++ handle all of this, it also means that you aren't going to necessarily be creating multiple copies of the same data over and over just because you need to change it in one place or another, leaving stray copies sitting around taking up space and causing, eventually, memory leaks or other things of that nature.

So how do you take advantage of this great function, then? You can do it through the usage of 'pointers.' Pointers are a relatively obtuse concept to actually comprehend, but once you get them, they become rather easy to grasp and work with.

So, essentially, you understand by now that when a variable is created, a place is cleared out in the computer's memory for that specific value to be stored. You can actually work with the specific location in the computer's memory where that something is stored in C and C++.

There are two primary pointer operators that you need to know: the *unary* (*) operator, and the *reference* operator (&).

The unary operator is used to declare a pointer variable. Pointer variables can store an exact reference to an address in memory.

The reference operator is used to refer to the address of a given variable.

You assign the *unary* operator variable to the address of a given variable using the reference operator. From here, you now have a pointer to that *exact location* in memory. This means that no matter what, when you alter that variable, you are altering the data at that exact location in memory, meaning that the variable is being directly manipulated.

This is useful for passing arguments between functions. When you pass arguments to a function, the value of those arguments is only copied over, and this means the exact values aren't passed. Therefore, if you change the value of a variable in a function from one form to another and you aren't using pointers, the value in the original function won't actually change, only the value in the secondary function will change, which is practically useless for changing variables outside of your main function.

Here is an example of using a pointer to change the value of a variable:

int i = 3;

int *p = &i; // creates pointer which points to address of i

*p = 6; // changes value at the address of i to 6

printf("%d", i);   //   this would print 6 since the value of i is now 6

Conditionals

It's now that we should start to get into one of the fun parts of the chapter, 'control flow.' Control flow is, more or less, the notion of giving your program the ability to make different decisions based upon the active state of any different number of variables.

In other words, you can make your program take different paths depending on what is happening at any given point in a program.

This is accomplished through the use of expressions, but before we talk about expressions, we need to talk about the concept of *Booleans*. In the next chapter, we'll be talking a bit more at length about *Booleans* and how they work in the context of C/C++, but for now, we're just going to do a cursory evaluation of them.

So, basically, *Boolean* values refer to either truth or falsehood. That is to say that a *Boolean* value may be either true or false. In C, there is a convention that these be designated with a 'B' at the start of the variable name, that they be an integer, and that they are either set to '1' if true or '0' if false.

But the concept of true or false goes much deeper than just determining whether something is true or not. It has to deal with a much bigger concept, logic. Logic is what you're actually getting into when you start to deal with this realm of programming and learning to think logically is an important step to becoming a well-rounded programmer, whether you're thinking of working on Arduino or anything at all.

Why? Because computers understand raw logic. That is all they know, computation and logic. They can compare things, and that, in the end, is the vast majority of what they're doing under the hood.

However, logic also plays a rather large part of our day-to-day life. Logic is the simple act of evaluation and determination. It is through evaluation and determination that many different decisions are made.

In the end, the ability to decide whether or not something is true determines pretty much everything that you're doing. For example, for me right now, I'm internally thinking *"Is the chapter done? If not, keep writing."* You may think to yourself in the morning, *"If I'm out of milk, I will go get groceries this evening."* You prepare your cereal, and you're not out of milk. Therefore you will not go to get groceries that evening, or at least not because you are out of milk. (There's another caveat here to deal with raw logic, but it's beyond the scope of this book, so I digress.)

This sort of evaluation forms the basis of many decisions that you make on a daily basis. True or false relations are how you base your own decision-making processes, generally.

Computers are very much the same way. You can actually give them the ability to make their own decisions based on any given number of variables. This is one aspect of control flow, 'decision making' it is also referred to as 'conditionals.'

The ultimate goal of a conditional is to evaluate an expression. Anything that happens thereafter is just a consequence. Expressions are established through things called *Boolean* operators or 'conditional' operators. We have the following as examples of these:

- **x == y**

  Evaluates whether x is equal to y.

- **x != y**

  Evaluates whether x is *not* equal to y.

- **x > y**

  Evaluates whether x is greater than y.

- **x < y**

  Evaluates whether x is less than y.

- **x >= y**

  Evaluates whether x is greater than or equal to y.

- **x <= y**

  Evaluates whether x is less than or equal to y.

In addition to these, you can chain a selection of statements through what are called 'logical' operators:

- **!(statement)**

  Evaluates whether the statement within is *not* true.

- **(statementA) && (statementB)**

  Evaluates whether both 'statementA' and 'statementB' are true.

- **(statementA) || (statementB)**

  Evaluates which of the statements are true, both 'statementA' and 'statementB' may also be true.

You can likewise chain logical operators together through the usage of parentheses to create larger logical statements, though after a bit it may be handier to break it down into smaller conditionals.

Now that we know how to set these sorts of expressions up, we now have to tackle the other looming question, 'What does one actually do with these concepts?'

Well, this is where we start to really get into the first major part of decision making, the 'if' statement.

If statements, at their most basic, allow you to check a certain statement. If the statement turns out to be true, then the code that is written within the if statement will be executed. If the statement turns out to be false, then the statement will be skipped over.

Let's say, for example, that we wanted a code that would evaluate whether the number of guitars was 2. Here's how we would write that.

```
#include <stdio.h>
int main()
{
        int numberOfGuitars = 2;
        if (numberOfGuitars == 2)
{
        printf("There are two guitars.\n");
}
        return 0;
}
```

One thing you'll notice in this program, however, is that there's a little bit of a lack of nuance. For example, the only time something will ever happen is if there are 3 guitars. If that's not the case, then nothing will happen flatly, and the program may as well not exist.

This is where we start to get into a topic that I like to call 'passive vs. active' conditional statements. You'll understand why they're called as such in just a second.

Passive conditionals are conditionals that occur passively. That is to say that their condition is evaluated and if the condition turns out not to be true, then the statement simply doesn't execute. Whatever happens next in the program happens, and the world effectively goes on.

The active conditional sets up a stark contrast to this. When you use an active conditional, you're setting up a catch-all statement; a blanket set of code that will always execute regardless of whether or not the condition is met. This means that the program cannot escape the consequences of your if statement. If the statement turns out not to be true, a certain set of code will execute without exception.

There are different scenarios in which you may need these functionalities, and those specific scenarios will become more clear to you as you work with programming more and encounter a greater number of scenarios overall. However, for the time being, let's just work on creating an active conditional.

The scenario for creating an active conditional is essentially defined by the addition of something called an 'else' statement. Else statements come immediately after the if statements and are used to say that no matter what happens, *some code* will execute. You can read if-else statements as, *if condition x then y, otherwise z.*

Here is our code above modified so that if there were anything other than 2 guitars, the program would tell you:

```
if (numberOfGuitars == 2) {
        printf("There are two guitars.");
} else {
        printf("There are not two guitars.");
}
```

There's one last element to add to all of this. What if you find that for one reason or another, you need to be able to check more than one condition for truth? What do you do then? Well, the answer, simply put, is to utilize what is called an 'else if' statement. Else if statements allow you to check a condition if the first condition turns out not to be true. It goes between your if statement and your else statement.

Let's say that you wanted to change the program we've written so that it evaluates whether there are less than 2 guitars, 2 guitars exactly, or more than 2 guitars. How would we do this? Well, let's first think about it logically.

The first thing we want to check is our primary condition, this makes our code easier to read. Modulations on the condition come afterward. Our primary condition is whether there are two guitars exactly. That will be our primary if statement.

Now, let's think about this for a second. The other thing that we're checking is if there are more or less than 2 guitars. Obviously, if one of these isn't true and there not being 2 guitars isn't true, then the 3rd option must be true by necessity and logic. So we can assume that one of these will be our second condition, we'll just say *less* than 2 guitars, and the other will be our else condition. Therefore, we'll check if there are two guitars exactly or if there are less than two guitars. If neither of those is true, then obviously there must be more than 2 guitars, so we'll act accordingly in our program.

We can program this like so:

```
if (numberOfGuitars == 2) {
        printf("There are two guitars.\n");
} else if (numberOfGuitars < 2) {
        printf("There are less than two guitars.\n");
} else {
        printf("There are more than two guitars.\n");
}
```

And with that, we've cemented the logic of conditionals a little bit. This was an important first step in truly understanding control flow. From here, it's time that we move on to the other major aspect of control flow, known as 'loops.'

Loops

Loops are a very intuitive thing to understand, but they're also
rather foundational to a huge amount of programming logic.
You'll understand this more and more as you work with them.
However, not only are they foundational to programming
logic, but they're foundational to logic in general.

Understanding how loops are foundational to logic, in general,
will help you to understand better why they're important to
programming, so we're going to spend a moment thinking
about that. Do you realize that you use loops constantly? You
may not think about it, but a lot of the things that you do are
just things repeated over and over. Just because you aren't
constantly thinking about the fact that you're looping doesn't
mean that a certain action isn't being repeated and slightly
changed.

Take saying the alphabet aloud, for instance. If you wanted to
say the alphabet aloud, you would start at position 1, which

would be the letter 'A.' You would open your mouth, say the letter A, then move forward to position 2, which would be position 'B.' You would repeat this until you land on the final letter. At this point, you would consider yourself to be finished with saying the alphabet.

In all of this, there is a regularity, find your position, say the letter at the position, move forward one position. This is just one example of how one may loop in their everyday life without thinking about it.

A more practical example is typing. To type a sentence on a computer keyboard is actually a loop because there is a reiterated set of conditions that may or may not change every time. The evaluation of which letter needs to be typed, the striking of that letter, then moving on to the next letter in the word.

Looping allows you to do things over and over and also to iterate over sets. C loops, in particular, are quite interesting because they're based on the Boolean conditions that we've already covered earlier.

There are two main kinds of loops in C and C++, 'for' loops and 'while' loops. Both serve a fundamentally different purpose but function in what is mostly the same manner at their core.

The first one that we will cover is the simpler of the two, the while loop. The while loop is a loop which will run over and over for as long as a certain condition is met. When the condition is no longer met, the loop will be terminated, and the program will move on to the next part of the code.

The syntax of a while loop in C and C++ is like the example below, and this also ports to other languages such as Java and Python:

```
while (condition)
{
        // code goes here
}
```

The most common utilization of the while loop is to create what is often called a 'game' loop. Game loops are so-called because they follow the logic of a game, that is, a game will generally follow the same pattern on both sides until a certain condition is met, usually a win or loss condition. Once this condition is met, the game is considered to be over, thereby terminating the loop. This sort of logic is often mirrored in loops in C++ and C and is a perfect fit for the while loop. Generally, if you need something to happen over and over for as long as a certain condition isn't met, the while loop will be the way that you want to go.

There are also *for* loops. For loops are far more interesting, and they also have a far more complicated structure. The purpose of for loops is iteration, which means going over a certain set of data piece by piece. They have an incrementing variable built right into them, which is just a show of how this particular function is provided for.

For loops follow the following syntax:

for (initialize iterating variable; condition to run; iterator step)

{

    // code within

}

Let's say that we wanted to print the numbers from 1 to 10 out to the console using a for loop. We would do this like so:

for (int i = 1; i<=10; i++)

{

    printf("%d\n", i);

}

This will start at 1, then loop for as long as the variable 'i' is less than or equal to 10. On every run through the loop, i will increment by one. It will also print out the number 'i.'

Loops in C and C++ aren't terribly difficult, and you'll gain a greater appreciation for when to use each kind as you press forward, so just keep pressing forward!

Functions

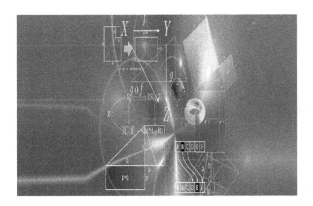

The last thing that we really need to talk about in this section
is the idea of 'functions.' What are functions, exactly? Think
back to high school or introductory college mathematics where
you would deal with things like $f(x) = y$. That is the basic idea
of a function, something which can give back a certain value
and or perform a set of statements. The primary difference
between mathematical functions and computer functions is
that computer functions don't necessarily have to return a
value, and computer functions don't necessarily have to return
an argument.

The basic syntax for a C function is like this:

*dataType functionName(arguments) // arguments not
necessary*

{

// code goes here

*return value; // not necessary if function is
void type*

}

Functions can be of any data type, and when you get to C++ and start developing classes, they can also be of class types too. Moreover, they can be of a type called 'void.' If a function is of the type 'void,' it does not have to return a function necessarily. A function must otherwise return a value of its given data type. This returned value can either be stored in a variable or manipulated directly.

The key appeal of functions is that they may be called from within other functions. This allows your program to remain very modular and easy to read. It also ensures that you don't have to write the same code over and over. This is an unnoticed perk, and it simply means that when you need to rewrite code, you don't have to change it in multiple places throughout your program. You can simply rewrite it and have that be it.

This saves you a lot of time and effort as the programmer because it means you don't end up refactoring most of your code because you need to change how something works.

Here's an example of a C program where a function to calculate area is called from within the main function:

```c
#include <stdio.h>
int calculateArea(int length, int width)
{
        return length * width;
}
int main()
{
```

```
    int area = calculateArea(7, 3);
    printf("%d", area);
    return 0;
}
```

This brings our chapter on C to an end. We will spend the next chapter building on our knowledge with C++.

Chapter 3:
C++ Programming to
Take You Further

The last chapter was actually a bit more of a crash course on programming in general, especially the logic concerning programming. We didn't spend a terribly long time dealing with in-depth concepts like console input and output because of the fact that as an Arduino programmer, they simply aren't as necessary as understanding the core logic behind the programming and being able to apply the concepts when you see them in Arduino projects or when you need to write your own code.

Don't worry though, in this chapter, you aren't going to have to learn a whole new set of skills. C++ is actually an extension of C. Developed first as 'C with Classes' by Bjarne Stroustrup in the 1980s, C++ is the attempt to add compatibility with object-oriented programming paradigms to C. This means that by and large, C and C++ were historically cross-compatible. Though the constant development of other language means that they have diverged from the higher level programming concepts, they still are, at their roots, intrinsically intertwined. For example, you still can import C headers into a C++ file with minimal compatibility issues.

For this reason, you can rest assured that anything we covered in the last chapter still applies in this chapter. The syntax for everything you did in the last chapter remains the same (aside from C-fundamental operations like printing to console), which means that variable declaration, array declaration and initialization, function declaration, loops, and so forth all pretty much remain unchanged. Marked differences are observed in this chapter.

Remember that the primary goal of all of this is to give you enough of a basis in programming that you can ably program for Arduino and carry out any projects that you want to. The intent is to make sure that you can easily read all of the programs that you look to for inspiration, or at least can make out their core functionalities in code.

In this chapter, we're going to be discussing C++ concepts that build on top of what you already know. These are things which you will most likely see referenced in other projects, especially when projects grow to a certain size or ambition beyond just tinkering.

Booleans

We've talked a little bit about this before, but the first thing we really need to cover is that in C++, *Booleans* were actually added to the language as a primitive data type, meaning that they're built into the language and don't function as an object. (This will make more sense in a second.)

In other words, there is now a *Boolean* data type that you can use, and it is created in the same way that *ints*, *floats*, and so forth are. The keyword is *bool*.

This is one of the major additions that you should know. They were also added to later versions of C but they were added to

C++ first so, for posterity, I've decided to add them to the C++ section. It's also easier to digest if we break *Booleans* down into two sections because now we get to talk about *Booleans* as a value.

Remember how in the last chapter, we talked about how a *Boolean* refers to a true or false, and how conditionals evaluate as true or false? Well, you can now store the values of conditional statements as a *Boolean*. This means that you can make a statement like:

bool continueRunning = userHealth != 0

This would evaluate whether 'userHealth' was equal to 0 and then return the result as true or false to the variable *bool*. Additionally, you can now create *bool* functions which return *Boolean* values, and you can store the results of these to *Boolean* functions.

In the end, you can also just store raw truth/false data: *bool continueRunning = true or bool continueRunning = false, respectively.*

This also plays a major part in allowing you to conceptualize *Booleans* as truly just being another value and another thing to be compared in the context of the grander program.

Namespaces

Namespaces are another new addition in C++. While they're not entirely new, they are certainly noteworthy and used in a far greater capacity. Namespaces allow functions, variables, and things of that nature to be grouped together to be referenced from within a program.

Strings

Among the many things that C++ brings to the table is one of the most prominent, a full-fledged string class. Thanks to this class, part of the STL, also known as the 'standard template library,' a collection of different interfaces compatible with C++ intended to massively extend the functionality of the language and programs written within it. C++ strings have a far greater level of nuance and power than their C counterparts. Don't misunderstand, of course, C strings were very good for what they do, but they did have their limits. For example, you have to predefine the length of a string as a character array, and there could be no active and reflexive modulation of the length of the array. This meant, necessarily, that strings had a fixed length.

Also, given the nature of strings, many operations which are made rather easy with C++'s string library were far more difficult, unwieldy, or unpredictable.

The biggest part here, though, is that strings now have a standard form. The first thing that you do is include the *string* library, like this for instance:

#include <string>

From there, you're able to define string variables like you would an *int*, *char*, or *bool*, with their value being the set of characters encased in quotation marks, like this example:

string greeting = "Hello there!";

You can also perform arithmetic functions to concatenate strings. All of this goes to show the beauty of another C++ concept known as 'operator overloading,' which is the redefinition of the language's operators within the definition of a class so that they can describe the way how the instances of the class may relate to each other. We'll discuss what this means more, in-depth, momentarily when we get to the object-oriented section.

You can also, thanks to the fact that they're defined as objects, access their member functions. This is yet another thing that will make more sense here in just a minute when we get to the object-oriented part, but that's kind of the crux of this whole chapter as well as the most confusing part, so I'm taking a moment to build up to it.

Object-Oriented Programming 101: The Basic Ideas

So, here is where we start to define a lot of the core ideas that we've been building up to throughout the book. This is also where one of the dual-purposes of this book starts to become clear. While this book is a great asset for people who want to learn Arduino programming, it also gives you a great amount of knowledge in terms of programming and computer science theory that you can port to any language or project that you may want to do, with a little brushing up on some additional concepts. (For example, file input/output, advanced console input/output, development of graphical user interfaces, so on and so forth.)

Nowhere is this truer than in object-oriented programming. In practical college courses, object-oriented programming is normally reserved for later on in the semester because it's a big topic and tends to intimidate people because of the sheer fact that it actually is a little complicated to comprehend. However, not only will you, in your Arduino programming, find this knowledge useful as you look at other people's programs and see how they implement their ideas, you'll find it useful if you should discover a love for programming in general and decide to spread that love for programming to other realms than just Arduino programming.

So here is where we have to quit with the exposition and get right to the lesson. What is object-oriented programming? What makes it different? What are classes and objects, and why were they so important that right after C was developed, somebody had to come along and create C with Classes?

The answer to all of these is that object-oriented programming is, more or less, another programming philosophy. C++ was one of the first languages that were really implemented for mainstream use, and Java was the first language to be fully object-oriented. The object-oriented paradigm is fundamentally different in many ways from the paradigm established by other programming philosophies like functional programming or procedural programming.

Where the emphasis in other forms of programming is based on the ability of a program to perform tasks in a certain way, object-oriented programming began to hit the mainstream as computers got far better and programs became more sophisticated. It was more of an inevitable reaction than a chance movement. Programmers developed what they saw as the best course of action for programming.

Object-oriented programming isn't based around accomplishing a single purpose necessarily, but around a few different key concepts that allow the code to grow easily, be easy to manage, and be easy to build on top of.

So, in effect, what does this actually mean in terms of practical programming terminology? Basically, it means that object-oriented programming is based on the philosophy of breaking programs down and abstracting them as much as possible.

In fact, object-oriented programming as a paradigm was somewhat defined by the introduction of Java, with the following goals in mind, abstraction, encapsulation, permutation, and modularity.

Abstraction is the notion that a programmer shouldn't have to work extremely hard to do any one thing; it's the idea that the programmer should be moved away from the technology lying under the hood so that they can focus on actually making programs that do what they want to do without dealing with absurd amounts of boilerplate code. This rule is where C++ falls a bit short, but it's no big deal — this is just a staple of the functionality of C++ and the amazing number of things that you can do with the extremely powerful language. Reserve abstraction for the languages which benefit from abstraction; C++ has a set purpose to fulfill.

Encapsulation is the notion that systems should be ideally self-contained and that things should be grouped together. Like

how attributes should be grouped under the same umbrella
and therefore referred to by the same name. C++ doesn't
automatically provide for this concept, but it allows the
programmer to provide for it with relative ease.

Permutation is the idea that things may take several forms
throughout a program's design and execution, and that these
things may serve multiple purposes under the same essential
name and or function. For example, there may be two different
functions that take different sets of arguments but that share
the same name and the same core function, a concept known
as 'function overloading.' In C++, whenever something is
given multiple purposes dependent upon context, this is
known as 'overloading.'

Modularity is the idea that things should be broken down and
reused. That is to say, that a definition should go a long way,
and there should likewise be many definitions established to
make programming easier as a whole. Modularity essentially
refers to establishing a base for yourself in terms of code and
then being able to detach or attach other pieces of code to it
with ease.

So how are all of these concepts applied, in a practical way,
and then coalesced into some sort of common system?
Through the development of object-oriented programing
structures, chiefly 'objects,' and 'classes.'

Of these two, we're going to cover classes first. Classes are
foundational to object-oriented programming and are, in fact,
the thing which everything else in object-oriented
programming ultimately derives from, in a literal sense. A

class at its simplest is a grouping of different attributes and functions under a common name.

For example, let's say that we have a class called 'car.' All cars share a group of common attributes. For example, they have wheels, they have a production year, they have a top speed, they have a color, a make, a model, and so forth. Because of this, instead of defining attributes as variables for every single car individually, or even defining them as groups of disconnected arrays which, without some sort of indexing mechanic, could get rather confusing in and of itself, we could theoretically group all of these attributes together into something called a 'car' class. If all cars share these properties, then it stands to reason that any definition of a car will contain definitions for these properties.

Every car will additionally have common functions. For example, all cars will be able to go, to stop, to honk, and so forth. Since all cars have these functions, we could declare these functions similarly as a maxim, therein becoming attributes of cars themselves, such that every car should have a definition for these actions. We could also, in the definition of the car class, provide a basic definition for these actions that way we don't have to redefine them for every car.

This is the most basic idea of a class, the combination of a certain group of attributes under a singular banner such that the singular banner can ably represent the attributes of each, with the attributes being either defined by default in the class definition or defined when an instance of the class is created.

An object is just an instance of a class. Objects are all distinct from the moment that they're created.

A class may be defined like this:

class className {

    accessSpecifier:

    //variables and functions within

};

You can then declare an object of the class like the following:

className objectName;

From here, you can actually access the object's member data with a period. For example, if a 'car' class had a variable called 'doors,' and you defined an object of the car class named 'pontiacGrandAm,' you could access the number of doors like this:

pontiacGrandAm.doors

I used the term access modifiers, and you may wonder what those are exactly. Access modifiers determine what can be accessed from outside the class. For example, if something is private, it cannot be modified from outside the class or without methods defined by the class. (Get and set methods, for example.) Public data can be modified from outside the class, so a public variable can be modified like so:

pontiacGrandAm.doors = 4;

Whereas a private variable would have to have a function to change the variable defined within the class.

Protected data can only be modified by all inherited classes, which are beyond the scope of this book. They are generally bad practice, though.

With that, we've covered a lot of what there is to know about object-oriented programming. This should save you some grief in your Arduino projects and help you better understand what you're working with.

Chapter 4: Understanding the Arduino Framework

In this chapter, we're going to actually start looking at the code which fuels Arduino. At this point, we are assuming that you have your Arduino unit and you've got it set up and linked to your computer. This is the first step.

The second step is to get an Arduino compatible IDE. For most beginners and novices, the ones supplied by Arduino themselves will be more than enough. You can navigate to their website and either download the desktop IDE or use the web-based IDE. Either one will work perfectly fine.

So, from here, we need to talk about the structure of sketches.

An Arduino sketch has two basic components that make it up: the 'setup' function and the 'loop' function. Both are essential to the overall functioning of the Arduino sketch, and so you need to make sure that every sketch you run has them. Your sketches, of course, are not limited to just these functions, and you can expand with more functions at ease as we described back in the C chapter.

The Arduino 'language,' so to speak, is just an extension of C and C++, which means that C and C++ coding conventions will work within them, as well as all of the things that we described previously. This makes programming your Arduino unit relatively easy.

The Arduino 'language' is actually a library with various different definitions and functions that are tailored to the Arduino.

This is how the most basic of Arduino programs look, in terms of structure:

```
void setup()
{
        // code within
}
void loop()
{
        // code within
}
```

The setup function should be just after the declaration of variables at the start of your sketch. It will always be the first function that your Arduino unit runs, so pay careful attention. You must have your setup function, even if there is nothing within it.

You use the setup function to do things like initializing Arduino relevant variables, like your pin modes. In other words, any necessary setup that you have to do to get everything up and running, those functions should be called from within your setup function.

Do note that not necessarily all of your variables must be declared here. Variables should generally be declared within their primary function or in the global scope. If you fail to define a function at these levels, you won't be able to use it where you want it to. For example, if you defined a variable within the setup function, you wouldn't be able to use it within your loop function since it was defined within another function and isn't global.

The loop function does pretty much exactly what it sounds like: it loops over and over until the program is brought to an end. When the program finally is brought to an end, the loop ends. Programs are generally brought to an end by cutting off power to your Arduino unit, so there isn't much of a way to exit the Arduino loop function. This is the primary function of your program, and everything happens from here.

Consider the fact that when you program something like an Arduino gadget, it really is just looping some function over and over every second, even if that loop is just something like waiting to receive input and then responding respectively when said input is given.

In terms of actual Arduino code from the framework, there are a few that you really need to know at this point.

Constants

Constants are a foundational part of Arduino programming because they allow you to make comparisons or assign certain things easily. Constants are variables which are predefined and do not change. They can be used as references in other functions used within the language.

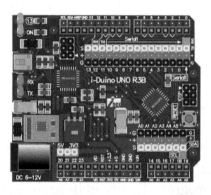

Two constants are 'TRUE' and 'FALSE.' This harkens back to the language on *Booleans*. TRUE here is defined as anything other than zero, where FALSE is zero.

Two more are 'HIGH' and 'LOW.' These refer to the voltage being given to the pin, and the respective pin levels. HIGH refers to a pin which is 'ON' and which is receiving 5 volts while LOW refers to a pin which is 'OFF' and is receiving zero volts. This is used most often when you are either giving or receiving data from digital pins.

The other two constants that you need to know at this point are 'INPUT' and 'OUTPUT,' which merely allow you to define the mode of something and whether it is for incoming data or outgoing data.

Functions

There are some different functions that are inherent to Arduino programming that we need to cover. While a large amount of Arduino functions will vary depending upon the gadgets you have and the project that you're specifically trying to tackle, there are nonetheless manifold important

The first is *pinMode*, which takes the arguments of *pin* and *mode*. Pin is the respective integer of the given pin, where mode is either OUTPUT or INPUT, as we just said. Therefore, it ties in perfectly to what we were just discussing with the constants. This function will always be called within your setup function.

The next is *digitalRead()*, which takes an argument of a given *pin*, either as a constant or a variable. This will read in a value from a given pin and return either HIGH or LOW, this indicates either true/false, on/off, or 5v/0v.

The next is *digitalWrite*, which takes the arguments of a pin as well as HIGH or LOW, which will essentially turn a given pin on or off.

The next is *analogRead,* which accepts an argument of a given *pin* and will take a value from the analog in pins. It will return an integer value instead of HIGH or LOW.

After that is *analogWrite,* which will take the arguments of *pin* and *value. AnalogWrite* allows you to write what is essentially an analog value to a given pin. The value can be from 0 to 255, and the size of the number will indicate how often the signal sent is either 5 or 0 volts; a larger number indicates that the charge will more often be 5 volts than 0 volts. This works in a wave manner and will, therefore, act as a means to regulate how much power is being sent to the given pin.

After the read and write functions is the *delay* function, which pauses the program. It takes an argument of milliseconds, either as a variable or a constant. It will cause a pause in that length.

Beyond that is *millis()* which just returns the number of milliseconds that have passed since the current sketch started as a long. This number resets after several hours.

After that are the min and max functions, which take two arguments both and return either the smaller or larger number respectively. They accept numbers regardless of data type.

After that is *randomSeed* which accepts a given integer as an argument. This creates a seed for a random number generator.

Beyond this are the two random functions. Given one argument, the random function will return any number from zero to the max value. Given two arguments, it will return a

number between the two numbers given. You must use
randomSeed before you use a random function.

The last two functions we need to cover are the 'Serial'
functions, which allow you to transmit serial data:

- *Serial.begin()* accepts an argument of the rate of
  transfer in bits per second. This is called in your setup
  function. The average rate is 9600 bits per second, so
  when in doubt, just use this.

- *Serial.println()* accepts an argument of any given data
  and will then print this to the Serial Monitor.

Conclusion

Thank for making it through to the end of *Arduino*, let's hope it was informative and that the eBook was able to provide you with all of the tools you need to achieve your goals, whatever it may be.

The next step is to start working on projects and learning from other people's Arduino experiences to learn the framework better and learn all of the amazing possibilities of Arduino.

Finally, if you found this book useful in any way, a review on Amazon is always appreciated!

Arduino

───── ❧❦❧ ─────

*Best Practices to Excel While Learning
Arduino Programming*

Miles Price

liable for any hardship or damages that may befall them after undertaking information described herein.

Additionally, the information in the following pages is intended only for informational purposes and should thus be thought of as universal. As befitting its nature, it is presented without assurance regarding its prolonged validity or interim quality. Trademarks that are mentioned are done without written consent and can in no way be considered an endorsement from the trademark holder.

Table of Contents

Introduction

Congratulations on downloading *Arduino: Best Practices to Excel While Learning Arduino Programming* and thank you for doing so.

Learning programming can be quite difficult. The purpose of this book is to act as a companion book to other books which have a focus on actually teaching you about Arduino programming. This book will focus in some capacity on larger programming concepts to make sure that you understand them, as well as how these concepts interconnect with Arduino and how you can take advantage of them to become a better programmer.

It will also give solid general advice for you as you attempt to become an Arduino programmer, such as things to help bolster your learning experience altogether. Assistance will be given in finding communities to help you out, and a long list of different tutorials and sample projects for you to either try out for yourself, emulate, or simply to act as inspiration for your own ambitions.

The truth is that learning programming can be challenging and daunting, and there is generally a lot to take in. Because of this, it's important that you have some sort of reference material that will help you to become a better programmer in the end and that will help you when things start to get a little heavy. It can be very easy to start to drown in the details when you're starting to program, especially with something as nuanced as Arduino.

Nevertheless, with this book in your hand, you're going to develop a firm grasp on a lot of different concepts and start to feel like you have a very solid idea of everything that you need to know to keep moving forward as a programmer. Along the way, you'll also build up a large base of support in the form of other programmers that are doing exactly what you're doing: trying to get better.

So relax - Arduino can be frustrating, and so can programming. However, with this book in your hand, you're going to have plenty of educational material to help you figure out exactly what you're doing as you go along.

There are plenty of books on this subject on the market, thanks again for choosing this one! Every effort was made to ensure it is full of as much useful information as possible, please enjoy!

Chapter 1:
Learn About Arduino

This is perhaps the best starting place for any. The best way to get started with learning about Arduino and learning how to be a capable Arduino programmer is to learn, beyond face value, what Arduino actually is, as well as what purpose it serves and what purpose it's necessarily *supposed* to serve. If you want to be a better Arduino programmer, then having some sort of idea of the origins of the thing itself will open your imagination up to the things that you can do with it.

More or less, Arduino first came around in the early 2000s when students at a design institute in Italy were trying to develop a low-cost microcomputer that would allow people to pursue many technical projects that would normally be prohibitively difficult or expensive for people who are less familiar with advanced electronics.

This was coupled with the development of easy to understand platforms that would allow people who otherwise would never really touch such complex hardware to have the opportunity to learn more about the complexity of hardware and software in an intuitive manner that would have a relatively low learning curve and enable them to get into tinkering as a hobby.

What resulted was a tool that serves as an amazing prototyping device. The Arduino is capable of allowing people to build easy prototypes of electronic inventions at little cost in terms of components. It also is relatively forgiving of a platform and allows people the room to experiment and tinker in a relatively low-stakes environment. At the end of the day, too, if something does go awry, the Arduino is low-cost enough that it's easy to replace.

However, the Arduino isn't just good for prototyping. Hobbyists would quickly pick it up and see it as a great catalyst for all sorts of projects that otherwise would be difficult to do. For example, there are projects such as a colored keypad that unlocks doors, which seems at first glance like something straight out of a sci-fi movie.

Basically what Arduino has allowed people to do is to take any gadget idea they may have and tinker with code and hardware until they have something that works for them in terms of their overall vision. In this capacity, there are few things better than Arduino.

Moreover, the actual language for working with the Arduino is relatively simple; many of the electronics which are compatible with the Arduino are very easy to use, and there is a large enough community that you can find support for almost any issue that you may have. (We'll talk more about this a bit later, though!)

All in all, in terms of a rapid prototyping tool, it is very difficult to beat the Arduino. However, it's also difficult to beat it in terms of a cost-effective solution for any gadget or trinket ideas that you may have floating around in your head.

Chapter 2:
Join Arduino Communities

There's little better that you can do for yourself as a new programmer than to join communities; there are few things for which this is more applicable than Arduino.

The simple truth is that Arduino is not easy in any way, shape, or form. In the hands of a hobbyist who is willing to learn, it can be an extremely powerful and interesting contraption capable of making your nerdiest dreams come true. However, this does have a precondition - you must be willing to *learn*.

However, not all learning comes from a book; in fact, most doesn't. You could spend all day poring through the pages of this or that book about Arduino or Arduino projects and still not really pick up much information if you aren't actively trying them out.

More than that, there's not really a way to ask a book a question when you get stumped. And believe me right now, you will get stumped: when you're working with Arduino, you're working with electrical circuits and a bunch of small doo-dads that you've most likely never tinkered with before. These are subjects that people quite literally go to college for and spend years studying, so it's not exactly to be expected that somebody who just picks up a board on the internet will be able to use it perfectly right away. On top of this fact, you also have to learn to program in one language or another if you want everything to go smoothly and you don't just want to rely on other people's code and their exact build paths and instructions.

Because of these reasons, there's no greater decision that you can make than to spend some time researching Arduino communities and joining one or two. There are several perks that come from joining Arduino communities.

The first is a constant source of inspiration. People are working on Arduino projects all the time, and there are constantly projects released that build up on the idea of an older project. This means that there's a natural sort of linear progression to the world of Arduino, and the people within it are deeply embedded in the hacking subculture. The hacking subculture is largely based on freedom of information and sharing what you make with everybody such that anybody else who enjoys tinkering can likewise start tinkering using

something you made as one of their starting points. This works
out for you in two ways.

It works out for you on one hand because you don't have to
worry about seeking out inspiration. There are a huge number
of projects that are there to show you what can be done and to
help you imagine what *could* be done.

It works out for you in another way in that if any of the
projects do particularly inspire you - which they will - you
generally can find a lot of information by the people who
created the projects which will divine to you the specific path
that they took. When you're just starting out with Arduino
programming and conceptualizing your Arduino projects in
general, this can be a pretty major deal, and it can be a major
source of help.

The second is a constant source of feedback and help. As I said
earlier in the chapter, there is no way to ask a book for help if
you get confused, and if it doesn't adequately explain to you a

certain topic, then you most likely aren't going to be receiving any additional information on that topic from the book. By having a firm idea of what communities are available for you to browse and also being a member of those communities, you can first search when you have a question and then ask if you don't manage to find a satisfactory answer. As I said before, freedom of information and helping newcomers out is a pretty major part of the hacking subculture, so people generally are very welcoming of questions from interested individuals.

Moreover, there aren't many better learning methods than learning from mistakes. If you start to integrate into some communities based on Arduino and programming, then people there will be happy to let you know when you could be doing something better, generally in a relatively tactful way. It is through these mistakes you make that you'll grow as a programmer and develop a far better technique than you would have had otherwise.

However, it is not only about learning from your own mistakes but also from the mistakes of others. For example, if you were to take the time to read other people's posts and look into their projects to see what they were doing and what others had to say about it, especially posts when somebody can't get something to work, you're going to learn a lot by analyzing their code as well as people's responses to their code. You'll be subconsciously learning the best methods for programming with very little effort on your part, just by simply paying attention to what others are doing and how others say that they could be doing it better.

Arduino: Best Practices to Excel While Learning Arduino Programming

The best part of all of this is that Arduino has a pretty massive following. A lot of people work with this technology, and every day, there are more who develop an interest in working with it. Because of this, there are a massive number of different forums out there dedicated to helping people like yourself either become inspired and post their projects or get help from others and in general, build a sense of community.

One of the most common is Hackster. Hackster is a place where people post their Arduino inventions, and people can react to them. Hackaday is a very common one as well. Either of these will give you a huge number of ideas and a generally large amount of experience looking at and understanding Arduino projects. As I said before, the projects generally also will be bundled with code and precise directions, should you want to either do one yourself or modify it for your own devices.

In terms of forums, there are a lot of options. One of the most popular and active is the forum hosted by Arduino themselves on the Arduino website. Here, people congregate and discuss everything from questions about programming to general guidance and advice on projects all the way over to general questions about electronics. There are even off-topic discussion sections where users can build camaraderie and rapport with one another outside of the contexts of pure tech babble (as fun as pure tech babble can be.) This means that the forum can in a way become your home away from home when you're working on Arduino projects, a keen source of guidance and friendship both as you attempt to pick up a daunting new hobby.

Chapter 3:
Learn the True Logic
of Programming and Hardware

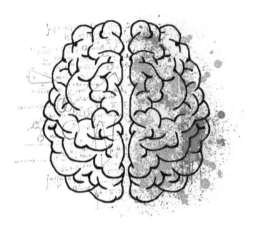

In the previous chapter, we talked a lot about what you can do to build yourself a support net, as well as the importance of *doing* so when you're trying to learn programming, especially with something so fickle as Arduino. In this chapter, we're going to focus on really reinforcing your knowledge of programming and hardware, as well as how they intertwine in terms of Arduino. This will enable you to make better programs because you'll have a much greater understanding of just what's going on under the hood in them.

Since you're working with Arduino, the chances are good that you're most likely working with C and C++, since these are the languages that the core Arduino library builds upon. However, since there are APIs intended to make pretty much any programming language that you can think of Arduino compatible, the lessons taught in this chapter will be purposefully vague so as to be applicable to any given language that you may be working with. Again, the purpose of this chapter is a reinforcement of main ideas and giving you new ways to think about things that you potentially hadn't before. In other words, where you may know vague programming essentials, the point of this chapter is to bolster your knowledge and teach you even more than you already know. This is all an element of building up a stronger framework within which you can work.

How Computers Work With Data

The first thing that we're going to talk about is how computers work with data. In this section, we're also going to be discussing the concept of memory and how it correlates to computers. It's an important topic worth diving into, especially when you're working with low-level systems.

Before you do anything else with a computer, there's one very, very important idea that you need to understand - everything that a computer does is one form of data manipulation or another. Even something so simple and plainly causal as the typing of a character into a word processor and the display of that character on your screen within the word processor. What you don't realize at any given point while doing so is that the program is doing a lot under the hood which you aren't recognizing; for example, when a character is entered into a word processor, the word processor's active *state* gets changed.

All programs work within a given *state*. This state reflects how the program is at any given moment, and any program's state is the result of various different things happening at the level of memory and processing. The most obvious is that the various states are stored as data within the computer.

0111100101011100111101011011100101110011110101101110010111001111101
1000110010101001010101100011001010100101010110001100101010010
1010110110101011011011101011011010101101101110101101101010101011
1110101110011111110110111010111001111111011011101011100111111110
0001010100100001011111000101010010000101111100010101001000001011
1001010101010101010100100101010101010101010100100100101010101010
1111100111111011001000111110011111110110010001111100111111011001
1110011110101101110010111001110101101110010111001111010110111
1110010111001111010110111001011100111101011011100101110011111010
0001100101010010101011000110010101001010101100011001010100010101
0101101101010110110111010110110101011011011101011011010101101100
1010101110011111110110111010111001111111011011101011100111111101
0010101001000010111110001010100100001011111000101010010000101111
0010101010101010101001001010101010101010100100101010101010101010
1110011111101100100011111001111110110010001111100111111011001
1001110101101110010111001110101101110010111001110101110010111001
1100101110011110101101110010111001111010110111001011100111110101
0001100101010010101011000110010101001010101100011001010100101010
0101101101010110110111010110110101011011011101011011010101101100
1010101110011111110110111010111001111111011011101011100111111101
0010101001000010111110001010100100001011111000101010010000101111

There is not one application in the world that is not built upon changing states; such is simply impossible. The program would be practically useless, and even the launching of the program would be a change of state within the operating system, even if not within the program itself. Moreover, variables that affect the state outside the program are altered constantly, so the state of the program at 10:49:36 PM is fundamentally separate in terms of instance from the state at 10:49:37 PM by simple cause of the fact that this is an altered variable at some point on the computer. It is impossible, except at the most rudimentary of levels - the turning off and on of an LED light by a button press through an Arduino program, for example - to escape the reality of changes of state. Even Arduino constantly reflects changes of program state through the fact that it has a constantly looping function within it.

So how do computers view states? What is a state, and how small can it go? In a rather abstract sense, states can go as low as the singular variable - for example, any variable has a given state that it remains as until altered.

What maintains these states? What determines these states? A greater understanding of programming at any level requires a thorough answer to these two questions.

The first thing that we need to talk about is the maintenance of data and states. How are these maintained? The simple answer is that these are maintained through storage, saved to be later manipulated by the program. There are two main methods of state and value maintenance, where a value is inherently considered a state because it's a static representation of some sort of data: these are the *hard drive*, which is used for long-term storage of data that will need to be accessed at a later point, and *random access memory*, which is used for the storage of short-term variables or variables which don't necessarily need to be stored on the hard drive.

Understanding how random access memory works is a major part of learning to be a better programmer, and doing so can, in fact, be a major boon to your ability to program ably. Random access memory essentially works by setting apart extremely small sections of data that can be altered in size and allocated as need be, as well as freed up and dismissed. It is the prime catalyst to actually being able to work with and manipulate things in your programs.

Perhaps a better question is how this applies to Arduino programming. However, this really doesn't need much of an explanation; when you're working with electronics, you are generally working with states. For example, an LED light has two states - on and off.

Moreover, an in-depth program - for example, one which is designed to read vital levels from a plant and then triggers the release of water accordingly - will be massively utilizing data, which is then intended to be manipulated either by the programmer or by the program itself.

So how does one build on this sort of notion? And more than that, what makes it important to us as potential Arduino programmers?

One of the primary ways in which this is important is the fact that, again, you are most likely using C and C++. The very nature of these languages is very low-level, meaning you have the ability to work directly with memory, to send pointers around, and so forth.

If, for the record, you don't know what pointers are - pointers are essentially things which *point* to a direct place in the computer's memory so that the data which is stored there may be altered directly. It's a relatively simple concept, but it can be hard to grasp at first.

However, beyond that, when you're working with the Arduino, you're not working with a very sophisticated system; knowing how data is manipulated within the system and, moreover, how it's stored within the confines of the system can lead to you have a better understanding of the manifold ways in which you can actually treat and manipulate the data therein.

Values and Variables

At this point, we're going to drive home a few factors about a couple key programming concepts. The first of these is *values* and *variables*. Often, programming books will teach you data types but not give you a lot of information as to what any of that actually means.

Given that the most prominent languages available for use today, especially within the context of Arduino programming, are either directly C, and C++ or C/C++ derived (such as Python, Java, C#, and so forth), we're going to be looking within the context of C-style values and C-style variables, as well as how both of these are handled.

In the last section, we looked into a bit more detail as to how computers handle data. What we didn't discuss is *why* they handle it in such a way. There is a relatively simple answer to this, though: computers cannot think. They cannot parse, and they cannot reason.

Computers are good at what they are named after: computing. And, in effect, this is essentially all that they are really doing at any given point: handling various computations and moving this or that value around to make some sort of change in the context of the larger program.

In the end, though, things get a bit more complicated than that: computers don't really have any concept of anything other *than* numbers unless you create an interface that allows them to have a concept of things at a level greater than this. This interface has been created many times over, by now, but that still doesn't necessarily mean that at the actual deep-down level of the computer that it understands it in any greater capacity than this.

However, computers don't even really understand things in terms of numbers: they understand them in terms of binary code. That is, a sequence of ones and zeroes that are understood by the computer to represent certain numerical values. The computers can parse these binary codes and perform mathematical operations on these binary codes. This creates the crux of the computer's processing, which is carried out by what is known as the central processing unit or *CPU*.

Programming languages, even at their most basic level (which is assembly programming, the language used to speak directly to the computer's processor and RAM), are designed to make it so that people don't have to simply work within the confines of binary code. More and more intricate systems are developed, and these systems define new systems which then reflexively define new systems still.

This is true especially for languages such as C and C++, as well as their derivatives in turn. These languages actually are renowned for their closeness to the computer's internals despite the fact that they are relatively easy for people to read. This can make it easy for one to work with them and really creates an abstract level for the programmer to work with.

However, this doesn't mean that these underlying concepts still aren't being practiced, they're simply being masked. So when you work with data and values, the computer is still parsing the information that you're sending it as more pertinent and complicated information than it's leading you to believe. All things will be eventually boiled down to ones and zeroes.

All things, too, within a computer, correlate to three things important: a number, a binary equivalent, and a space in the computer's memory.

This is where this aspect of the lesson starts to build on the previous part of this chapter. An intricate understanding of the interplay of all of these concepts will allow you to really start to comprehend the multiple levels at play in terms of a computer's internals, which will then transfer to your Arduino programming with relative ease.

So let's talk about this a bit more: when I say that all computers work within these confines, what I mean is that all values that your computer might interpret are eventually understood in this sort of manner as well. That is to say that if you were to use a *char* variable, your computer would interpret the ASCII character not ultimately as a character, but first as a character, then as assembly code, then as a number, then as binary.

These binary things are stored in terms of things called bits. Bits are the storage medium of your computer and are the way in which data is held and managed. Your random access memory automatically stores and recognizes things in terms of bits.

So what is the key point of all of this? That your computer doesn't actually understand what you're working with. This is why one data type is often incompatible with another data type, for example, or why certain data types can hold more data. Take, for example, the *integer* against the *long*.

The integer, in C programming, is 4 bits per the standard. This means that the binary code which can be stored in that bit can represent numbers up to and as large as around 32,000, with the capability for negative numbers being the same numbers being conversely negative. Meanwhile, the *long*, though still an integer, has more bits of storage reserved to it - 16 bits, exactly. This means that the binary configuration that can be stored for this number is larger, meaning that larger values can ultimately be used and determined here.

Some other things are taken into account, as well - unsigned values eschew one spectrum of binary numbers for another, despite taking up the same amount of storage in terms of bit space.

Understanding this is a key milestone in understanding how and why computers parse data in the way that they do.

This raises another question - what is a *variable*? The book will make the assumption that the reader knows what a variable *is*, but do you know how a variable truly *functions*?

A variable is, more or less, a reservation of space. When you declare a variable, you set aside a bit space of a certain designated size within RAM, the size being designated by the type of the variable. This is why you can often cast something of a smaller bit size data type to a larger bit size data type without corrupting the information, but you generally cannot cast something of a larger bit size data type to a smaller bit size data type without having the value change. (A cast, if you are unaware, is the changing of a variable's data type to another.)

When you refer to the variable, you refer to that specific location in the computer's memory, or rather the value which is stored at that location.

So what does all of this mean to you as a programmer, and what's the point of going in-depth on this? Well, the first is that there is the off-chance that you aren't coming from a language where data types are actually explained. For example, in a language like C++ or C, you are required to state data types, and they are, in fact, a major part of programming in these languages. If you don't understand how data types work in a conceptual way and their relation to memory, then you aren't really going to understand a lot of what's going on with your variables in these languages.

More than that, a lot of books - as I said - will gloss over this sort of important information in favor of a much lighter covering on the topic which doesn't actually tell you a whole lot in the way of understanding the overarching topic of data types and variables. Even still, there are some things that aren't discussed here because I'm trying to stay language-neutral and just give a theoretical understanding of these topics. One such example would be the way that variables are passed between functions in C/C++ versus other languages, where variable values are copied, but the address of the variable itself isn't actually passed in C/C++. This means that an altered variable in another method in C/C++ will lead to the true value of the variable not actually changing, where in a language like Python, for example, the variables will be passed in reference to their address, meaning that a changed variable in another function changes the variable in the original function.

Truth and Logic

Here we get into lessons which are actually rather foundational to programming but that aren't very much discussed: logic and truth. If you want to be a professional programmer and get a degree, most degree plans will require you to study discrete math for the reason that discrete mathematics discusses many different topics which are core to computer science in a rather abstract way, like trees and graphs and, above all, logic.

All things which are carried out by a computer are ultimately just methods undertaken to verify whether something is true or whether something is false. After all, this is all an equation is in the end - the discovery of truth on one side of an equation in terms of the question on the other side, which makes math almost linguistic in its properties.

Having a keen understanding of logic and truth is imperative if you want to work on large projects that go deeper than simply pushing a button and having something happen. It's true too that when you're working with truth and logic that you start to see patterns that you might not otherwise.

In the end, having a solid understanding of truth and logic is what really causes you to *think like a programmer*. Programmers are constantly thinking of how something can be done or interpreted in a logical and concise manner, rather than getting bogged down with details of aesthetics. Programmers are, in that sense, pragmatists, such that they want their programs to do exactly what they need to do and they don't want them to waste their time.

This is hardwired into the programming tradition by virtue of the fact that computers solely understand logic and truth. At the end of the day, they are mathematical machines, and math is comprised of nothing but these two concepts. The ability to interpret, expand, and work within these two concepts is absolutely paramount to becoming a good programmer.

The first thing that we should talk about is logical statements and what they are, as well as how they work.

All statements have some degree of logic to them, and all statements can be parsed in a logical way provided that they are semantically sound. The idea of logic studies is to reduce the semantics of a sentence or phrase to those which are most necessary to convey a key point, then analyze it to say if it is effective at doing so.

Take, for example, this sentence:

If I pay you $20, you will wash my car.

This sentence is very semantically sound. It is composed of the premise and the conclusion - *if I pay you $20* is the premise which implies the conclusion *you will wash my car.*

Let's look at yet another example:

If it rains today, I will not go to the park.

This sentence too is semantically sound and rather barebones. There is an implied *then* after the comma in both of these example sentences. Either sentence is based on the idea of a premise which implies a conclusion.

This is the basis of logical statements in programming, but not necessarily logical operations.

Note that with both of these, we can take the premise and then break it down even further in a logical sense so that we can actually analyze the true meaning of the sentences. Let's look at the first.

If I pay you $20, you will wash my car.

First, let's detach the premise to analyze it:

If I pay you $20...

Now, let's take the *if* clause out of it:

I pay you $20.

This is the core of the statement. There are a couple implications here, first that there is a *set amount to be paid* which is equivalent to $20, the second that the amount *is being paid*.

Understand that this relation of subject to action is a key part of logical statements and logical premises. Using these, we can set up nearly Socratic logical statements:

If I pay you $20, you will wash my car.

I paid you $20.

Therefore, you wash my car.

Note that this only sets up a unilateral relationship between the premise and the conclusion. It means that if the premise occurs, the conclusion *will* happen. However, in logic and computers alike, it doesn't necessarily mean that the conclusion won't just happen anyway. For example, somebody may just start cleaning my car without paying them; because there is no established relationship there, they are free to do so. However, there *is* an established relationship anchoring the premise to the conclusion, even though there isn't one going the other way. In this capacity, if I pay somebody $20, they will wash my car per our agreement. They may wash my car even if I don't pay them $20, but if I pay them $20, they may not *not* wash my car.

The premise here can be looked at in both programming and mathematical terms as an *expression*. An expression is a statement which necessarily implies some sort of relationship between two things.

From a programming standpoint, we can look at this in one of two ways. The first is that we take the statement in a literalistic way:

```
if (amountPaid == 20)
        you.washCar();
```

However, this isn't the correct way to break it down logically. This only sets up a relationship according to the *amount paid*, not necessarily to the action taking place at all. We can assume that this isn't a time for a numerical expression but rather for a boolean expression:

```
if (I.havePaid == true)
        you.washCar();
```

So this illustrates an important lesson: logic is not easy, and sometimes the most immediate solution when analyzing a premise isn't the necessary way forward.

Let's look at a statement where we *can* distill a premise into a numerically comparative expression. Let's take the statement *if I have zero cans of Coke, I will go to the store.*

First, note once more the way in which this sentence functions logically: the premise sets an anchor to the conclusion, but the conclusion may occur with or without the premise. I have only set up a situation where if I'm out of Coke, I must go to the store; however, I am not *required* to have run out of Coke to go to the store, and I may still go to the store anyway.

Let's parse the premise again. There seems to be only one clear way forward:

```
if (fridge.cansOfCoke == 0)
        I.goToStore();
```

This is a case where numeric analysis of a given premise is the right way forward. This also leaves the statement open-ended.

This is where we have to discuss another topic that's often underlooked: the usage of if statements in terms of logic and program flow. If statements are an incredible utility, and this book makes the assumption that you know in a proper sense how they work. It also makes the assumption that you know how *else* statements work. I've always referred to the difference between the two as a *passive conditional* versus an *active conditional.*

The difference between these two is of great importance when it comes to logical flow, and it seems like nobody ever takes a methodical approach to discussing when and where to use one or the other. This can be of great confusion to new programmers who don't quite understand the structure of logic yet - especially when younger - and don't seem to have their heads on, so to speak, when it comes to questions of optimal logical programmatic flow.

Passive conditionals are so-called because in no way does the logical flow of the program depend upon them. In one way or another, they are completely and entirely exempted from the normal logical flow of the program. That is to say that if a certain condition isn't met, a passive conditional - in reference to a conditional which only consists of a given if statement - may be completely skipped over by the program. The logical flow of the program would then bear no consequence as to whether the given statement even existed in the first place.

These have their uses, largely in terms of catching single conditions that should initiate a given action. Later, in the algorithmic section, you'll see one such event: a variable should be swapped with another, but only in the case that the first variable is larger. If this isn't the case, however, we don't actually want our program to do anything.

These so-called event triggers are important to flow in many programs. In video games, for instance, keystrokes are listened for and reacted to with event triggers the vast majority of the time. Other chain reactions within the program are handled methodically through if/else statements and entity states to handle things like animation in respect to these keystrokes.

In Arduino programs, passive conditionals find a lot of use in the sense that states are used rather extensively. Take the state of a given button connected to a switch. Were this button pressed and in the on position, a current would be given. Arduino would, therefore, register the button as being in the *on* state. One could implement in Arduino's running loop that if this button is in the on position, something may happen.

Active conditionals, on the other hand, are intrinsically attached to the logical flow of the program. Active conditionals are if else statements or if else if else statements; in other words, statements which have some sort of backup clause should the given conditions be found to be false.

These are great for making logical decisions with your programs. They allow you to start decision branches and are a key foundation to things such as neural networks. Decision branches give your program a crazily high amount of interactivity in a logical sense and make it able to do way more than it would be able to otherwise.

Understanding when to use a passive or an active conditional is paramount to being a great programmer, but not every book takes care to make sure that you understand the logical differences between the two; they often will rush through this important part to get to discuss other things.

Loops

Loops are yet another thing which are incredibly important and foundational but are often understated in ordinary programming books. The thing is that the authors of programming books tend to, in my opinion, undervalue the weight that these concepts have in true relation to the gravity of the program. It's for this reason that I'm going to spend as much time as I can expanding upon these concepts so that you understand when these things are to be used in terms of your program's flow and direction.

So, let's start by talking about loops in a rather abstract way. Loops are very much a common occurrence, but we don't always appreciate their utility. Loops are prevalent in things which happen every single day and, indeed, in most actions that you take. Any sort of repetitive action - repetitive in the sense of literally repeating, even if you don't notice it - is a form of a loop.

Let's consider something as innocuous as scrolling down your Facebook feed. Even this is a loop in a certain way. You look at a post, then you evaluate the post, determine whether you want to like it or comment on it (or block the person who made it), then you move on to the next post. The process repeats ad infinitum until for one reason or another, you decide that you'd no longer like to look at Facebook posts. The loop is therefore considered complete.

Loop logic applies to a whole lot of different things that we never quite take the time to appreciate. However, appreciation of loop logic in its most raw form is important if you want to become a better programmer. Again, the purpose of this chapter is to look at things which are normally glossed over by other programming books.

Before we think on the logic of every loop, though, let's just delineate what loops there *are*. There are *while*, *do while*, and *for loops*. In languages such as C#, there are also *for each* loops. All of these loops serve diametrically different purposes within the context of program logic, but from a detached view, they tend to look and act very similarly. It's only through experience that one really realizes the difference between these loops in a logical sense.

However, I'm going to try to explain the difference between these loops in a logical sense because any large-scale project that you do is inevitably going to involve loop logic and it's important that you as a programmer can comprehend which you should be using and when. Additionally, if you are a new programmer than you may not even realize that these loops can be used in such a way as they're about to be presented, or you may not have even thought of them that much. In this sense, this portion will give you the information necessary to think like a more seasoned programmer.

Let's start with while loops. A lot of introductory programming courses like to say that while loops and for loops are interchangeable because they aren't willing to bog you down with information about the practical usage of the two; while they are, in many cases (especially when you're starting out) interchangeable, there are many cases where they are *not*, in fact, interchangeable, or at the very least shouldn't be interchangeable in the name of good practice.

This is because the real-life application of these loops is diametrically different from the textbook application of these loops.

Let's take while loops, for instance. While loops, in terms of logical function, are simple. They have a chunk of code within them which will execute repeatedly until the condition given is no longer true. Hence, the code runs *while* the condition is true.

while (condition) {
         // code within
}

This is pretty simple at face value, but it can be a bit denser of a topic when you consider its actual utility. For most functions where you're iterating, a for function would carry far more utility. So what good does the while loop actually do?

Well, the utility of the while loop comes through in the fact that it can be used efficiently and easily to constantly check a *boolean* condition. That is, it shouldn't be used for iteration but rather for carrying out a specific action for as long as something else *hasn't* happened.

This kind of logic is often called the *game loop*. This is a reference to the fact that in games, a similar procedure will often take place over and over until a certain win or loss condition is met, at which point the game loop is considered over (because the end condition has been met.)

Meanwhile, while functionally similar, the *while* loop actually differs a lot in practical usage from the *do while* loop. While the do while loop is frowned upon in some circles as being a poor choice in terms of programming convention, it still serves a functional purpose. The do while loop is used to execute a certain block of code, then continue executing it for as long as the given condition is met.

The thing is that much of the time, the condition *won't* be met in practical usage, so this actually differs quite a bit from the while loop. More often, the do while loop is used generally when the condition needs to act as a safeguard. The code *must* execute once, but if something goes awry or isn't quite as expected, the code will continue to execute until whatever issue is ironed it.

```
do {
        // code goes inside
} while (condition);
```

And both of these differ largely in practical usage from the for loop. The for loop is used to iterate over sets, especially arrays, whether those be the arrays themselves (e.g., an array of integers) or an array within a class definition (e.g., iterating through single characters in a string or iterating through a string array after a string split function). The for loop sees a great amount of its utility in the fact that it is specifically intended for iteration.

Languages such as Python make this perfectly clear in the fact that their for loop structure actually demands a range to iterate through. There are a number of other languages which follow this example. Unfortunately, most C-style languages typically don't make the cut, leaving themselves a tad bit vague.

However, if you really break down the declaration of a for loop in a C-style language, you begin to see its utility as an iterative loop. First, you actually declare an iterative variable. This holds a massive parallel to the declaration of an iterative variable in Python for loops, but it's much clearer in Python what the exact intention of the iterative variable is. Afterward, you define the condition for which the loop runs. This is where you get to define your effective range as the difference between the maximum end point of your loop and the minimum start point denoted by your iterative variable. You then can designate an iterative step, which is normally ++ or --, though could really be anything so long as it's something which moves at the same rate every time.

This gives us the following structure for for loops:

```
for (iterative variable declaration; condition; iterative step) {
        // code within
}
```

While Pythonic languages have the somewhat clearer variant like so:

```
for iterator in range_definition:
        # code goes here
```

For loops generally serve a common purpose across languages, though, which is the key point to take home; most languages have some form of a for loop. The thing that differs is the implementation of the range definition.

For loops, too, have their limits; this is where *for each* loops come into play. For each loops are used to iterate through high-level objects. They're often used in conjunction with high-level collections such as lists, vectors, or dictionaries. They are composed of an iterator object of a given type; as the collection is iterated through, you may then use the iterator object as a placeholder to access member data of every element within the given collection. This is wildly useful but often understated. It also bears a strict logical difference from the other forms of loops, so it is never given its fair time. The general syntax of a foreach loop is like so:

```
for/foreach Object o in List {
        // code goes here
}
```

While some languages manage to get by without a foreach loop, they do massively simplify the process of iterating through objects, as well as ensuring that things go smoothly within the loop in terms of object definitions.

Object-Oriented Programming

This book assumes that you know things about programming, or at the very least have another source to learn them from and are using it as a supplement. Because of this, while it would be very simple and perhaps even easy to start rambling on and on about what object-oriented programming is and what objects and classes are and so forth, this book is written based on the assumption that you know what they are.

Rather, the intent is to help you to become a better programmer in general by explaining the logical and theoretical side to things that are often skipped over. This pattern isn't going to change for this section.

Object-oriented programming is, nonetheless, quite important, and it's important that you have some sort of understanding as to what its purpose is in terms of programming paradigms, as well as the general design philosophy that goes into it.

You may be wondering, if you have any familiarity with object-oriented programing, why one would be interested in it as an

Arduino programmer; after all, Arduino is procedural by its very nature... right?

Wrong, actually. More nuanced and sophisticated Arduino programs will often have very in-depth structures that are not only defined but complemented by object-oriented programming paradigms. In essence, object-oriented programming is the idea that all things in programming should be abstracted and modular.

Essentially, things should be moving towards readability and reusability. Additionally, a huge focus should be placed on the ability to maintain code over a long period of time and easily make changes to it without having to go into long refactoring cycles.

So, moving on, there are some key object-oriented concepts that many books tend to gloss over. We're going to focus on these more in-depth in a logical sense here.

The first is *overloading*. Overloading is a major factor in object-oriented programming, but it's usually treated in passing or as something to learn "on the job." Overloading is the concept of things being made multi-purpose. That's it. While this doesn't seem incredibly detailed or articulate, there's not much more to it than this.

There are a few different forms of overloading, but the most prevalent is *function overloading*. Function overloading is when you give more than one definition of a function to the same name, which allows the function to execute in different manners dependent upon the arguments given.

There also is *overriding*. Overriding is another form of overloading. It's a very important concept, though. Before we discuss overriding, we should stop to be sure that you understand what *inheritance* is.

We assume that you know what classes are; however, it's worth noting that classes can *come from* classes. This is called inheritance. What happens is that a new child class is defined, and this class inherits the various methods and variables from its parent class, in addition to any newly defined methods and variables.

Often, in these cases, it will be necessary to redefine a function from a parent class. In this case, one should use function *overriding*. This is when you use the override keyword with the same function and arguments to essentially tell the program that this object needs to use its *own* function instead of its parent's version of the function.

There's one more object-oriented concept that many books neglect to cover, and that's the issue of the object-oriented *ethos*; not every program will require object-oriented programming. However, with how much it's talked about, people often make it seem like object-oriented programming is the end-all-be-all of programming. You shouldn't go around defining classes when there isn't any need to.

However, chances are that there *will* be a need to at some point for you as a programmer, especially when you start working with really complex Arduino programs. In these cases, remember that the object-oriented ethos revolves around readability and modularity. At no point should a class definition or something of the like make your code more difficult to understand. It should be easy to add to or remove from, and it should be easy to change at a moment's notice.

With that, we've covered a lot of the inherent logic behind programming and how all of it applies to Arduino programming. In the coming chapters, we're going to be discussing further methods that will allow you to take your Arduino programming experience to the next level.

Chapter 4:
Spend Time Thinking Outside the Box (and the Arduino)

In the previous chapters, we've spent a lot of time talking about programming concepts and how they specifically apply to Arduino programming. In this chapter, we're going to talk about how creative thinking and spending time away from Arduino programming both might enable you to be a better Arduino programmer in the end.

This may not make a lot of sense, but the fact is that both of these ideas have a lot of credence. No masterful painter ever got to their mastery by working simply with oils, though they may strongly *prefer* to work with oils. The same applies here: without thinking outside the box and working outside of your comfort zone, you're going to be missing out on a lot of different things that would lead you to become a better programmer and a better Arduino builder in general.

Here's a simple fact for you: all of creativity is based on the way that the brain processes inputs and outputs. Although there is some variety of spontaneous components, you can only ever invent things which are based on those things you've already learned or those things you've already been made aware of. Your ideas will almost always be based on those inputs that you've already dealt with in the past instead of being based on things that are spontaneously generated in terms of new ideas.

Arduino: Best Practices to Excel While Learning
Arduino Programming

Spontaneous generation of ideas can lead to really cool and abstract things, but even the most spontaneous ideas are based on learned stimuli, from a psychological perspective. In other words, no thought that you've ever had has been completely original, because all of your thoughts are formed by the world around you and the unique way in which you happen to process all of that information.

If you want to be a good Arduino programmer, you really need to not stop at Arduino programming. For example, the fundamental languages which power the Arduino language itself, C and C++, have been used for a massive variety of different utilities in the nearly forty years that they've been around. At some point in these languages' long histories, there has been something done that you've never even thought of, surely.

It is by taking in these inputs and getting this practice that you enable yourself to become a better programmer and do more.

I think that a good example would harken back to the phenomenon known as a Magic Mirror. Magic Mirrors are computer monitors which display information fed in by a Raspberry Pi, a microcomputer not too different from an Arduino through a tad bit more powerful and intended for different purposes. The monitor is tucked behind a one-sided mirror such that the information on the monitor displays on the reflective side of the mirror. What results is a mirror that is incredibly science fiction becoming a science reality.

The thing is that while the project itself is simple, the logic behind the program really isn't; for example, to display the data, a modified version of the Chromium browser is used. Within that Chromium browser, a custom page is built using HTML, CSS, and JavaScript (to retrieve information from the web).

It is through the knowledge of how to make these different things happen that a project as ambitious as the Magic Mirror was made possible. If one didn't have the knowledge of how to modify and recompile the Chromium browser, nor if they didn't have the knowledge on how to build web pages using HTML, CSS, and JavaScript, the project simply would have never happened; it would have remained science fiction.

In other words, you may have incredible ideas, but actually being able to take action to make them happen is an entirely different beast altogether. One thing is for certain: building up the knowledge required to, for example, build web pages or modify and recompile a web browser then write a bash script to automatically launch it upon the operating system starting up are things which go well beyond the scope of hobbyist programming for the Arduino.

You can ask for the help of other people, but that will only get you so far and nudge you along a little at a time. So what's the other option, then?

All of this chapter has been building up to this: your ability to program Arduino sketches and to make your dream projects happen is based on you, not programming in Arduino at all.

Programming is a common set of skills that usually transfer across projects, but as an Arduino programmer, you generally are not building these skills in the optimal way. Reading books like this one is a start because they teach you the underlying concepts to all of the computer science mumbo-jumbo that you're being fed, which hopefully acts to help make things click a little bit. But there are a lot of bigger concepts that you aren't going to pick up just within your Arduino IDE. These are things like working with APIs, learning how to read documentation, learning how to create header files or libraries to make your programs more modular, learning in general how to be a better programmer.

These are skills which you gain through continually challenging yourself and trying to come up with new things.

And this has a little perk tacked onto the end of it, too: if you try to work on new things, you will be inspired more often. You'll learn how to do things and start having ideas that you wouldn't have had otherwise, because you'll be enjoying new experiences and getting all sorts of new inputs. When you think about things you've never thought about before, your brain interprets this as a good thing - as a learning experience. This will expand your mind and make you more creative, in turn making you simultaneously a better programmer and a better tinkerer.

So in other words, if you want to be a good Arduino programmer, one of the best things that you can possibly do for yourself is to start working on projects that aren't Arduino-based. You need to be exposing yourself to new things and challenging yourself to become better all of the time.

Chapter 5:
Learn the Implementation of Algorithms

In this chapter, we're going to discuss the implementation of algorithms in Arduino programming. Often, algorithms are understated in terms of their importance to Arduino programming, but using them, you're able to do many things that you wouldn't be able to otherwise.

An algorithm is, for lack of a better term, a way of standardizing a sort of procedure. We're going to be discussing two different types of algorithms and how they relate to Arduino programming, as well as discuss in both a theoretical and a practical sense how they can be implemented.

We first will look at the bubble sort algorithm and discuss sorting in relation to Arduino programming. Bubble sorting is the most simple form of sorting, but it will give you a decent look into algorithmic programming and a greater example of how algorithms actually are in practice.

The second thing that we will look at is a Bayesian probability algorithm which is important in statistical programming. Bayesian probability is also used to determine "true probability," which is probability that takes into account false positives and false negatives. We're going to be discussing why probability algorithms may be useful in Arduino programming and how you may find yourself using them in the future depending upon your various different projects.

Let's start by looking at sorting and thinking about when it could be useful to us as Arduino programmers. Sorting is the idea of taking some set of data and then filtering through it and moving things around accordingly. Let's say, for example, that we had an array of ten values. There are times where we may need to sort these. While there do exist certain functions in the Arduino library for getting the minimum or maximum of two values, there is no built-in sorting function for an array, and there's no built-in way to obtain the largest and smallest values within an array.

This is an introduction to algorithmic thinking more than anything else because Arduino is a perfect proxy to building bigger and better technological systems based off of concepts such as artificial intelligence and the internet of things. More than that, algorithms come up in complex programs and having some idea as to how to break down what an algorithm needs to do and then implementing it is a first important step to developing some sort of methodology for programming algorithmically.

The sample language for this example will be C/C++, but the key concepts will remain the same across any language. This is the first time in this book that we're not going to be using pseudocode.

Let's first define an array of 10 random values. You can make them whatever. Here are mine:

int numbers[10] = { 39, 63, 10, 70, 23, 34, 63, 13, 76, 34 };

This is the first important step. Afterward, we need to define the how our algorithm will work. Let's think about this for a second.

What a bubble sort essentially does is look at any given value in an array and compare it to a number either immediately before or after it. If the number before or after is larger or smaller (implementation can vary), then the two numbers will be swapped.

This might seem straightforward: you simply iterate through the array and perform checks to see if a given element is larger than another, right?

Not quite. If you used a single loop to iterate through the array, you're not actually going to be accomplishing much of anything. Instead, you need to use two for loops. The first loop will denote what we can call our *active position*. This will move through every element in the array one by one and perform the necessary checks and swaps until an *n*th element has been checked.

After that, you'll use a second for loop. This creates an *active integer* and compares it against every other element in the array. This is the loop of action. The other is the loop of iteration.

Within the loop of action, we must, therefore, create some kind of check mechanism. We can do this by comparing the active integer against another element in the array. If the other element is smaller, the two elements will swap positions. This means that the smaller element will be pushed towards the front of the array.

By now, we can assume that this means we need two functions: a *sort* function which will contain the logic of our sort mechanism, and a *swap* function which can perform the swap of the two integers given their addresses in memory.

We can implement these two like so:

For the *swap* function, we're going to want it to take the argument of two pointer addresses. Within the function, it will then define a temporary placeholder variable which we can call *i*. The placeholder will be used to store the value of integer 1. Integer 1 will then assume the value of integer 2. Integer 2 then assumes the value of the placeholder, which is the old value of integer 1, meaning integer 1 and 2 have now effectively swapped positions. Here is how I would define this function:

```
void swap(int *p1, int *p2)
{
        int i = *p1;
        *p1 = *p2;
        *p2 = i;
}
```

Easy peasy. The logic behind it is a little rough, but that's all an important part of the learning process!

Now, moving on beyond this, we're going to now work with our *sort* function. The sort function will create two iterative

arrays. It will accept the arguments of the array's size and the
array itself. It will iterate through these accordingly. Since
we're comparing in a forward manner, the active position
should only extend to the size of the array minus one element;
otherwise, when the last element in the array is reached, there
will be an element overflow error, and the program will crash
(if it executes at all.)

For the second for loop, we need to iterate according to the
size minus the active position minus 1.

Within the second for loop, we need to define an if statement
which checks to see whether the active integer is larger than
the number immediately ahead of it. If it is, then the two swap
positions, meaning we throw the memory addresses of the two
to the swap function.

Here is how I would define this function:

```
void sort(int myArray[], int size)
{
        for (int i = 0; i < size - 1; i++)
                for (int j = 0; j < size - i - 1; j++)
                        if (myArray[j] > myArray[j+1])
                                swap(&myArray[j],
&myArray[j+1]);
}
```

Again, it's not a terribly difficult algorithm, but it does require
a bit of thought and is a decent introduction to algorithmic
thinking if you've never done so before. To test this all, we can

create a program with our test array that will do all of this, then print it out for us so that we can see if all is in working order:

```
#include <stdio.h>
void swap(int *p1, int *p2)
{
        int i = *p1;
        *p1 = *p2;
        *p2 = i;
}
void sort(int myArray[], int size)
{
        for (int i = 0; i < size - 1; i++)
                for (int j = 0; j < size - i - 1; j++)
                        if (myArray[j] > myArray[j+1])
                                swap(&myArray[j],
&myArray[j+1]);
}
int main()
{
        int numbers[10] = { 39, 63, 10, 70, 23, 34, 63, 13, 76, 34
};
        int size = sizeof(numbers)/sizeof(numbers[0]);
        sort(numbers, size);
        for (int i = 0; i < size; i++)
        {
```

```
                printf("%d", numbers[i]);
        }
}
```

Your end program should look somewhat like the one above. If so, then you've succeeded.

The next thing that we're going to discuss in an algorithmic sense is probability using a very rudimentary version of Bayes' theorem.

So what exactly is Bayes' theorem, and why is it useful as an Arduino programmer? Well, Bayes' theorem in and of itself is a way of determining true probability of a given situation based upon the likelihood that something has happened in the past. It takes into account various given rates and then returns a certain dimension based on those rates.

For this, we can take two events: event X and event Y. We then have P(X) which is the likelihood of X, and P(Y) which is the likelihood of Y. $P(X|Y)$ is the likelihood of event X given that Y is true, and $P(Y|X)$ is the likelihood of event Y if event X is true.

Let's say we're trying to find the likelihood of event X given that Y is true, and we have data related to event Y is X is true. Bayes' theorem then allows us to look at it like so:

$P(X|Y) = P(Y|X)*P(X) / P(Y)$

In other words, the probability of event X given that Y is true is equivalent to the probability of Y given that X is true multiplied by the probability of X, then all of this divided over the probability of Y.

Bayes' theorem is a little difficult to grasp if you aren't looking at it in an intuitive manner. Take, for example, spam filtering, which is a rather common application of Bayes' theorem in the world of computer science.

Let's say that event X is the likelihood that the message is spam, and event Y is the likelihood that it contains certain words flagged as spam. P(X|Y) is the probability that it is spam given that it contains words flagged as spam. P(Y|X) is the probability that a certain word flagged as spam will be in a spam message. P(X) is the probability that any given message is spam, and P(Y) is the probability that the words within are flagged for spam.

Therefore, we can render the equation something like this:

The probability that a message is spam based on flagged words is equivalent to *the probability that the flagged words are in a spam message* multiplied by *the probability that a message is spam*, all divided by *the probability that flagged words are spam.*

This yields:

P(spam|words) = P(words|spam)*P(spam) / P(words)

This could be rendered algorithmically rather simply, and it's a very rudimentary probability equation. However, this does give us a solid starting point. The equation, too, can be mostly given over without much thought given to the conversion process.

For this, we're going to need just one function which returns *x given y* based upon *y given x*, *y*, and *x*. We'll call this function *calc_prob*. We will use this function to return a double value which will be saved to a variable and printed out to the console.

The finished code would look something like this:

```
#include <stdio.h>
double calc_prob(double ygivenx, double x, double y)
{
        return (ygivenx * x) / y;
}
int main()
{
        double spam = 3100, words = 6888, wordsgivenspam = 7000;
        double spamgivenwords = calc_prob(wordsgivenspam, spam, words);
        printf("%.2f", spamgivenwords);
}
```

With that, you've written your second algorithm. Probability algorithms become massively useful when you need your Arduino programs to be able to act predictively. For example, you could use your Arduino to model certain situations or react accordingly. While it's not powerful enough for hardcore number crunching, it will definitely be powerful enough for basic probability equations. This, for example, is nothing too intensive. So long as it can retrieve information to form a dataset, you can use much of the information in this book to make highly reactive Arduino sketches that could, ideally, change the world.

The purpose of introducing these two algorithms was to give you insight as to how algorithms might impact your programming and how thinking algorithmically can be a major boon to your ability to program in the first place. Consider that the ability to mentally process and break apart certain functions is foundational to being able to think like a programmer, which - in the end - is what this book is trying to help you do.

Conclusion

Thanks for making it through to the end of *Arduino: Best Practices To Excel While Learning Arduino Programming*, let's hope it was informative and able to provide you with all of the tools you need to achieve your goals whatever it may be.

The next step is to start using all of this information to better yourself as a programmer. Join communities and start researching projects that you think you would like to do. Progress now is within an arm's reach - make it happen!

Finally, if you found this book useful in any way, a review on Amazon is always appreciated!